W9-APU-876

THE TOTALLY BRILLIANT
WORLD
OF
PUZZLES

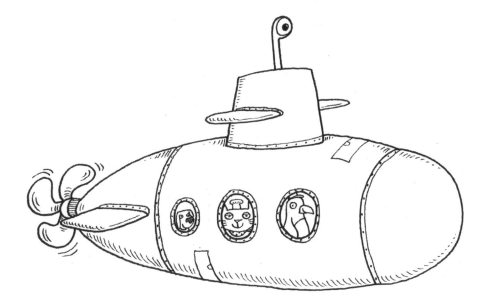

ARCTURUS

ARCTURUS

This edition published in 2015 by Arcturus Publishing Limited
26/27 Bickels Yard, 151–153 Bermondsey Street,
London SE1 3HA

Copyright © Arcturus Holdings Limited

All rights reserved. No part of this publication may be reproduced,
stored in a retrieval system, or transmitted, in any form or by any means,
electronic, mechanical, photocopying, recording or otherwise, without
prior written permission in accordance with the provisions of the
Copyright Act 1956 (as amended). Any person or persons who do any
unauthorised act in relation to this publication may be liable to criminal
prosecution and civil claims for damages.

ISBN: 978-1-78212-911-0
CH003767NT

Author: Lisa Regan
Illustrator: Beccy Blake
Editor: Kate Overy
Designer: Trudi Webb

Supplier 29, Date 0415, Print run 3998

Printed in China

ON SURFARI

Can you find each of the listed items in the main picture?

SHARK ATTACK

Write down the letters from the grid to find the top three most dangerous sharks in the world.

	a	b	c	d
1	F	O	M	H
2	K	U	C	L
3	E	A	S	W
4	R	N	G	D
5	B	T	J	i

a5 b2 d2 d2 c3 d1 b3 a4 a2

BULL SHARK

c4 a4 a3 b3 b5 d3 d1 d5 b5 a3

GREAT WHITE

b5 d5 c4 a3 a4 c3 d1 b3 a4 a2

TIGER SHARK

HEAD IN THE CLOUDS

Who lives up here in the clouds? Is it fairies, giants, or some freaky fantasy characters? You decide!

5

SUPER SPEED

Decode the message to find the name of one of the fastest production cars in the world. It's easy to decipher: A = 1, B = 2, and so on.

2 21 7 1 20 20 9

B U G A T T A

22 5 25 18 15 14

v e y r o n

ON THE LOOKOUT

Which of these groups of letters cannot be rearranged to spell MEERKAT?

TRAMEEK

KREMEAT

EKEMART

~~TREMERKA~~

KARTEEM

EATMARK

TRICK OR TREAT

Can you spot ten differences between these two pictures?

JUST FOR LAUGHS

Follow the instructions to find the answer to the joke.

Why does the Statue of Liberty
stand in New York?

ITS
WHEN
WISHES
ROOM
HOPES
WAIT
WORK
CAN'T
GOOD
STANDS
SIT
LIKES

WHAT
IS
NEEDS
SAYS
WILL
BECAUSE
WON'T
TOO
IT
FEELS
DOWN
SOON
WHITE
MOOD

Cross out any words containing -OO-.
Get rid of the words that start with W.
Lose all the words ending in S.

9

NO FISH

The oceans aren't only home to fantastic fish; there are all sorts of marine mammals, molluscs, and other creatures swimming around, too. See if you can find these ones hidden in the grid.

DUGONG
PENGUIN
SQUID
ANEMONE

CRAB
CORAL
WALRUS
PORPOISE

OTTER
SEA LION
MANTIS SHRIMP
CUTTLEFISH

P	E	S	U	R	L	A	W	C	P	M	W
D	A	N	E	M	O	N	E	R	O	A	A
U	P	E	D	H	T	T	W	A	R	N	N
G	E	P	U	S	E	N	A	A	P	T	E
i	N	C	G	i	P	O	T	T	O	i	N
M	G	R	O	F	E	i	T	O	i	S	O
P	U	T	N	E	N	L	D	T	S	S	C
E	i	T	G	L	N	A	C	U	E	H	U
S	N	O	B	T	T	E	N	R	G	R	T
Q	M	A	N	T	i	S	S	E	A	i	P
U	R	S	Q	U	i	D	E	Q	M	M	E
C	S	A	E	C	O	R	A	L	U	P	N

MISCHIEF MAKING

How many ice creams can you count in this room full of pesky pixies?

11

MISSING PARTS

Use the missing letters of the alphabet to
spell a vehicle that has only two wheels.

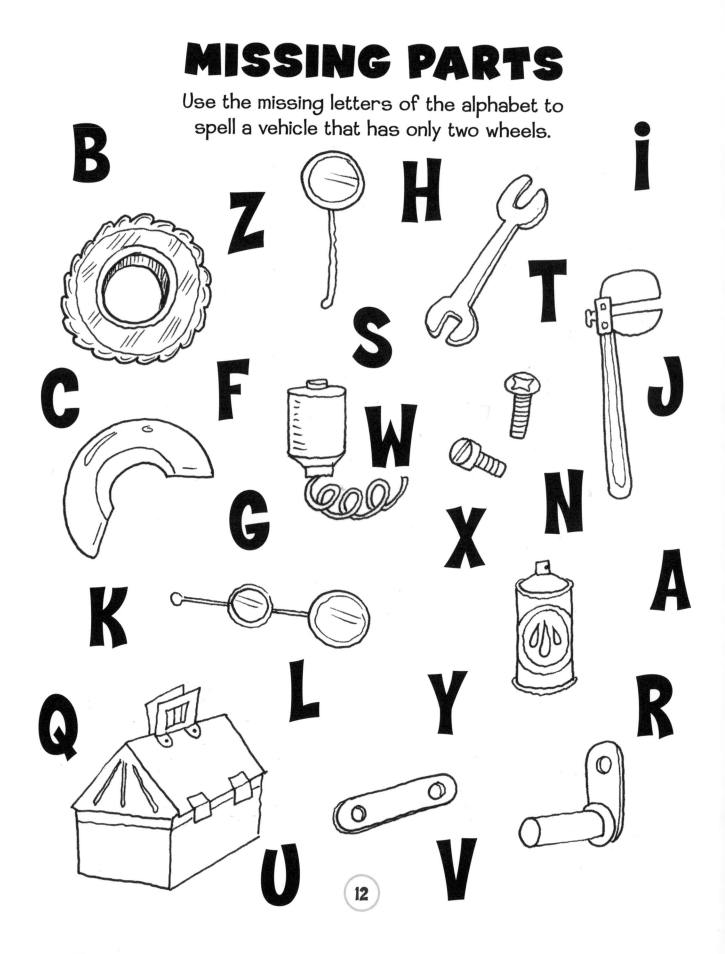

WALKIES!

How many words can you make from the letters in the phrase below?

I LOVE MY DOG

1. MODEL
2. _____
3. _____
4. _____
5. _____
6. _____
7. _____
8. _____

9. _____
10. _____
11. _____
12. _____
13. _____
14. _____
15. _____
16. _____

19

SPOOKY SCENE

Which four of the ghosts have slipped away in the second picture?

BUILDING BRIDGES

Do you know where these famous bridges are?
Cross out every other letter, starting with B, to find four
countries or cities. Then match each country to the correct bridge.

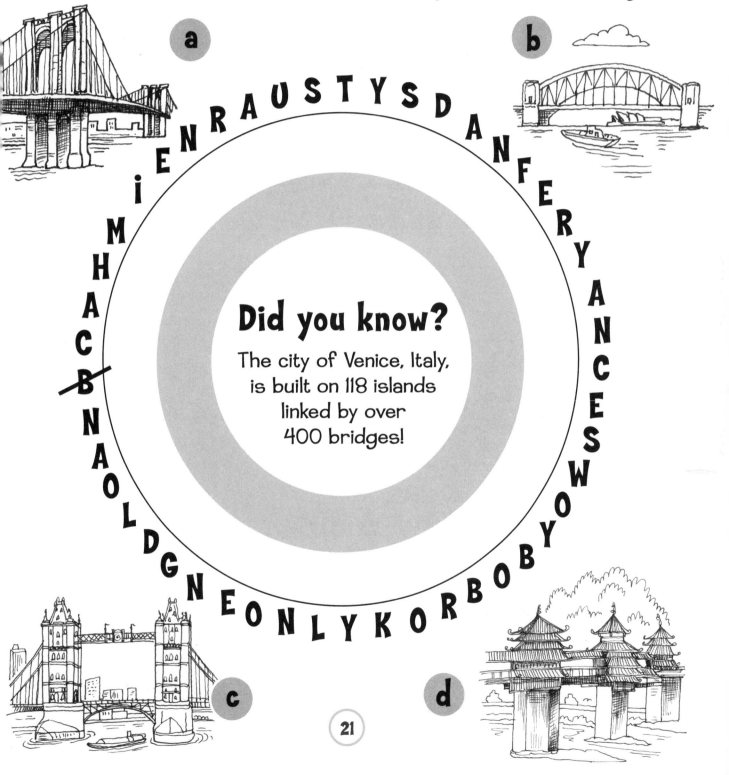

a

b

i E N R A U S T Y S D A N F E R Y A N C E S
M
H
A
C
B
N
A
O
L
D
G
N
E
O
N
L
Y
K
O
R
B
O
B
Y
O
W
S

Did you know?

The city of Venice, Italy,
is built on 118 islands
linked by over
400 bridges!

c

d

21

LOVING THE WAVES

Use the clues to figure out who does each sport,
and where they are from.

	ESTELLE	FLOYD	CARA
GREECE			
AUSTRALIA			
USA			

The Australian doesn't go diving.

Cara and Floyd both live in the northern hemisphere.

The wind surfer isn't from Greece.

Estelle's sport is motorized.

One of the girls is from Greece.

	ESTELLE	FLOYD	CARA
WIND SURFING			
SCUBA DIVING			
JET SKIING			

MYSTICAL CREATURES

One of these magical unicorns is slightly different from
the others. Can you spot which one it is?

 a
 b
 c
 d

 e
 f
 g
 h

 i
 j
 k
 L

 m
 n
 o
 p

ZOOM!

What numbers are missing to add up to 100 each time? Fill in the blank for each vehicle to make each one go at 100 miles an hour.

CHEEKY MONKEYS

Can you draw more monkeys playing in the tree?

BOOM!

Which one of the fireworks is a tiny bit different from the others?

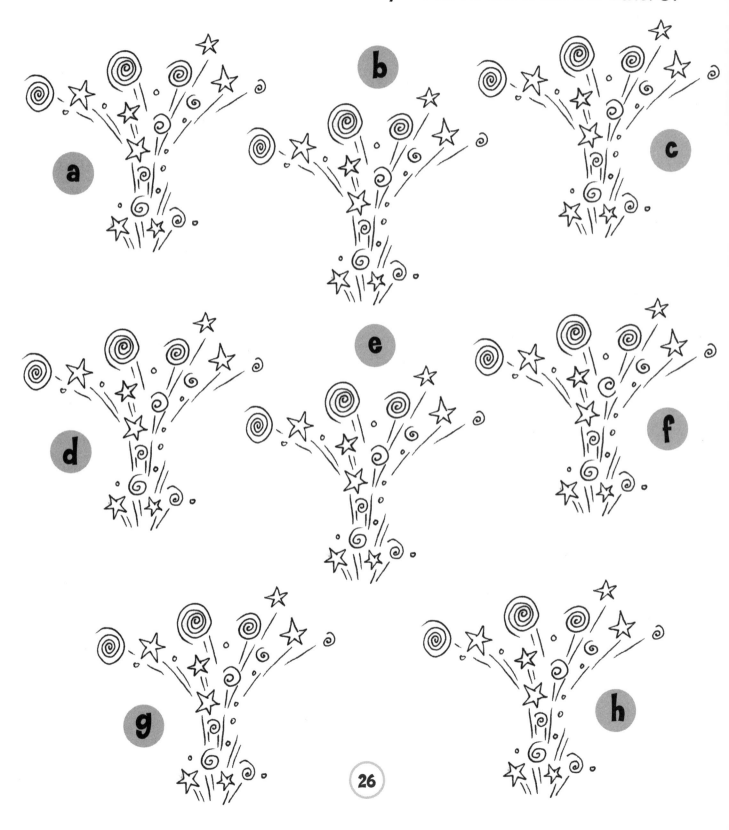

SLOWLY DOES IT

Help the tortoise find a path to the carrot,
following the arrows from leaf to leaf.

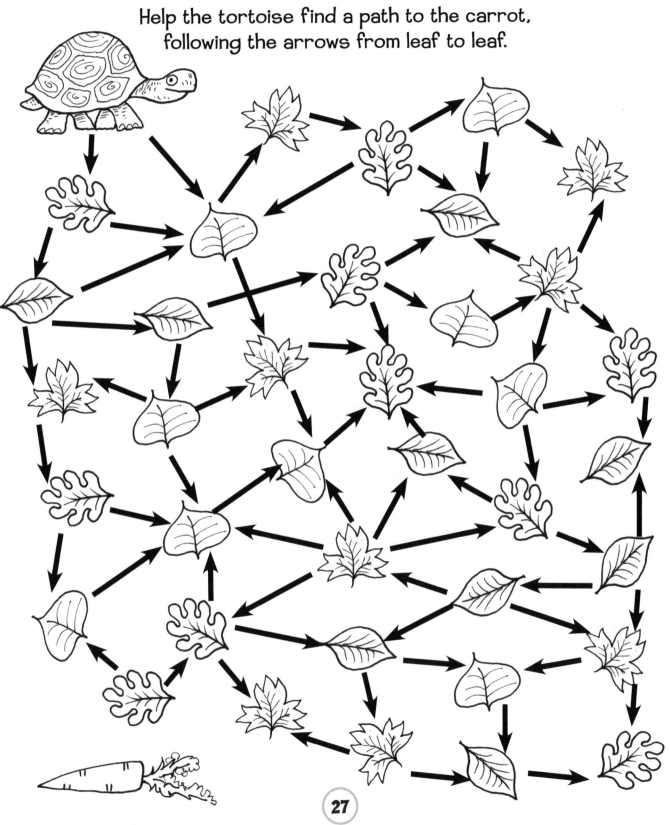

TREASURE TROVE

Can you spot each of these items in the main picture?

STEP UP

Write down the letters from the grid to help Steph
find out more about this Mexican pyramid she is visiting.

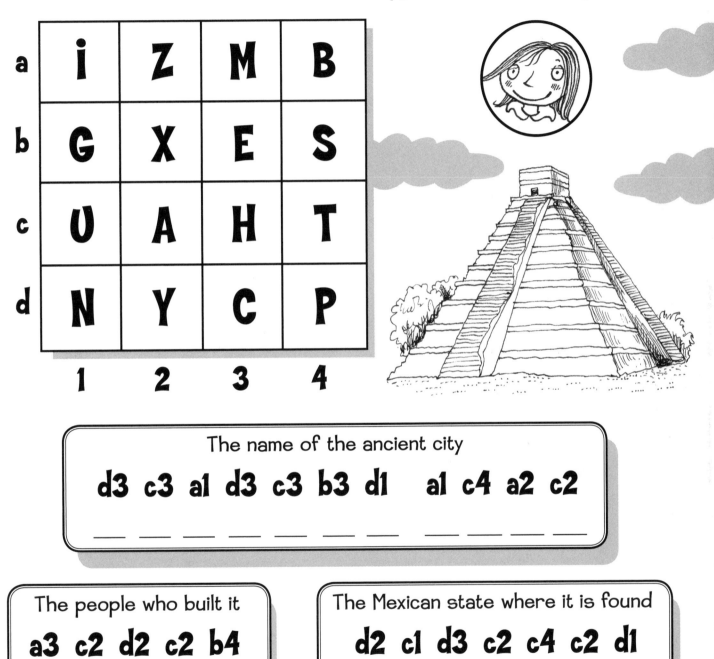

	1	2	3	4
a	i	Z	M	B
b	G	X	E	S
c	U	A	H	T
d	N	Y	C	P

The name of the ancient city

d3 c3 a1 d3 c3 b3 d1   a1 c4 a2 c2

_ _ _ _ _ _ _   _ _ _ _

The people who built it

a3 c2 d2 c2 b4

_ _ _ _ _

The Mexican state where it is found

d2 c1 d3 c2 c4 c2 d1

_ _ _ _ _ _ _

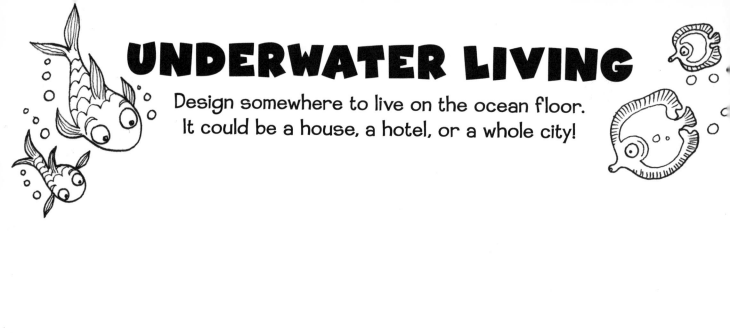

UNDERWATER LIVING

Design somewhere to live on the ocean floor.
It could be a house, a hotel, or a whole city!

FIGHTING DRAGONS

Unscramble the coded words by reversing the alphabet, so that A = Z, B = Y, and so on. The answers are all countries that have St George, the famous dragon slayer, as their patron saint.

VMTOZMW

VTBKG

RHiZVO

VGSRLKRZ

KLiGFTZO

RMWRZ

FPiZRMV

31

ON YOUR BIKE!

Fill in the grid so that each row, column, and mini-grid has one of each bicycle accessory in it.

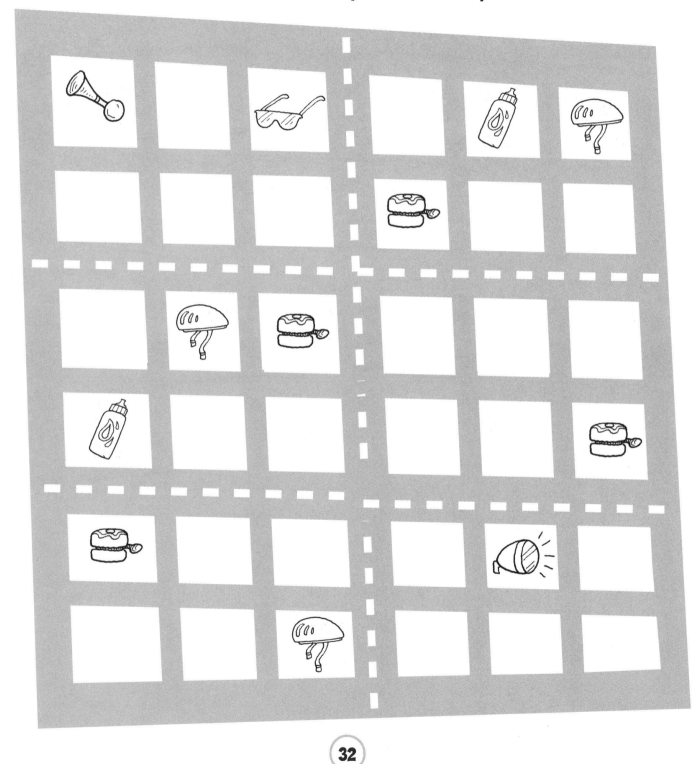

KING OF THE JUNGLE

Can you spot ten differences between these two pictures?

LIGHTS OUT

Sindy the spy needs to cut the right wires to disconnect the spotlight without setting off the alarm. Find the right set of instructions to see which wires she should cut.

Cut the black wires

Cut the bottom wires

Cut the striped wire

TOUR OF THE EAST

Asia is home to some of the world's richest history, most stunning scenery, and famous landmarks. Find all 12 of its biggest countries (by population) hidden in this grid. They can appear up and down, sideways or diagonally.

CHINA
INDIA
INDONESIA
PAKISTAN
BANGLADESH
JAPAN

PHILIPPINES
VIETNAM
IRAN
TURKEY
THAILAND
RUSSIA

V	C	H	T	J	P	T	H	A	L	G	N	A	B	T
i	i	H	T	H	A	i	L	A	N	D	V	i	U	H
N	P	H	i	L	i	P	P	i	N	E	S	R	S	A
D	A	S	S	N	N	P	A	S	V	i	K	i	S	L
P	K	P	H	i	A	A	P	U	E	E	N	N	R	i
V	i	E	T	N	A	M	P	R	Y	i	V	D	U	R
S	S	N	B	A	N	G	L	A	D	E	S	H	S	A
S	T	O	D	N	i	H	P	i	J	P	P	i	S	N
R	A	D	N	i	A	i	S	E	N	O	D	N	i	H
i	N	P	A	B	A	N	G	L	A	D	S	S	A	C

SHIPWRECKED

How many of each kind of fish are lurking in this shipwreck?

DO YOU BELIEVE?

Work out which letters are missing from the alphabet in each group, and then use those missing letters to spell out the names of four make believe characters. Are they real, or just imaginary?

AIR RESCUE

Which of these groups of letters is the only
one that can be rearranged to spell helicopter?

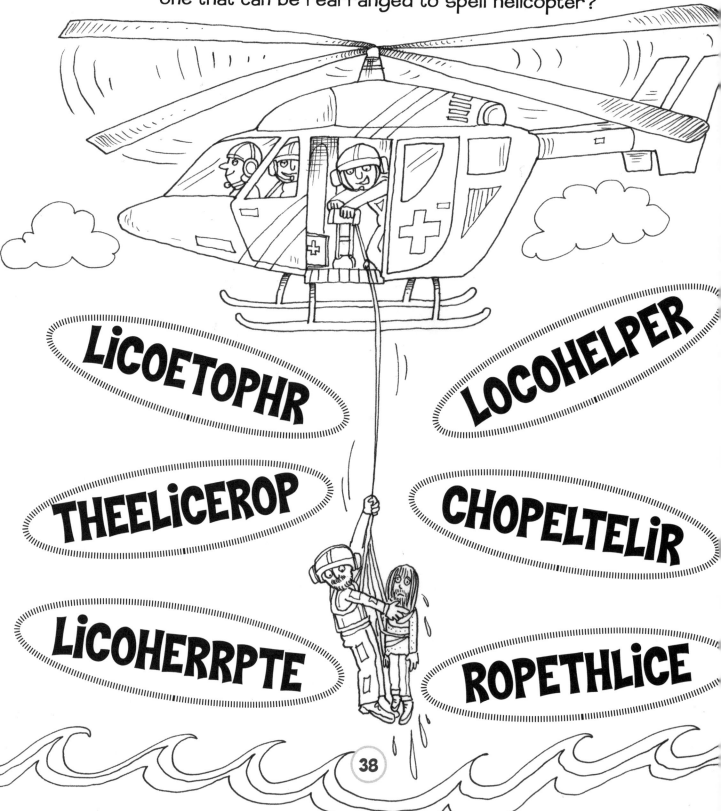

LICOETOPHR

LOCOHELPER

THEELICEROP

CHOPELTELIR

LICOHERRPTE

ROPETHLICE

I HERD THAT!

Which three small boxes make up part of the main picture?

GOING BATTY

How many bats have numbers that add up to exactly 100?

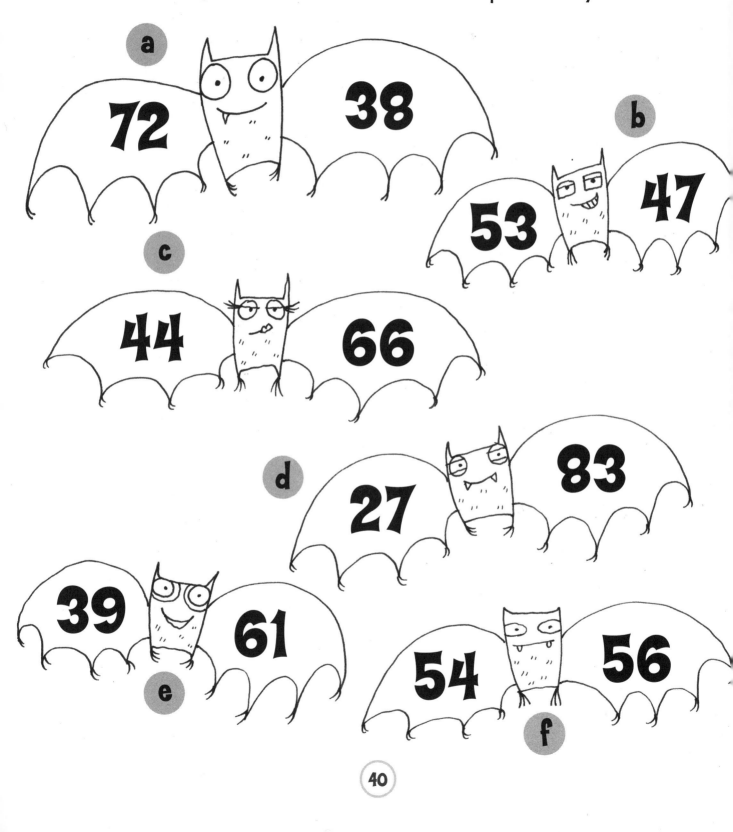

a) 72 ... 38

b) 53 ... 47

c) 44 ... 66

d) 27 ... 83

e) 39 ... 61

f) 54 ... 56

MAGIC SQUARE

Write the correct number next to each picture, using the clues to help you. If you get them all right, each row, column, and diagonal will add up to 15.

1 A country famous for its high speed trains.

2 The Netherlands are famous for these.

3 The world's biggest is in South America.

4 Its capital city is Rome.

5 The most famous of these are at Giza.

6 You'll have to travel across the Pacific Ocean to see these.

7 Its flag has six stars on it.

8 This monument is found in Paris, France.

9 The world's biggest are in the Himalayas.

SUPER SUB

Which of the silhouettes matches the main picture?

DRINK ME!

Can you spot one magic potion that doesn't match any of the others?

OFF ROADING

How many words can you make
from the phrase written here?

FOUR WHEEL DRIVE

1. DELIVER
2. _____
3. _____
4. _____
5. _____
6. _____
7. _____
8. _____
9. _____
10. _____
11. _____
12. _____
13. _____
14. _____
15. _____
16. _____

44

MORE AND MORE

Which new rabbits have appeared in the bottom picture?

IN THE DARK

Cross out every other letter, starting with L, to find a time when there are more hours of darkness than at any other time.

FRENCH TRIP

Ben has had a great week in Paris. Use the clues to fill in his diary with the sights he saw and the treats he ate each day.

MONDAY

TUESDAY

WEDNESDAY

THURSDAY

FRIDAY

SATURDAY

SUNDAY

He visited Versailles on the same day he ate tarte tatin.

On Monday he had mousse and on Sunday he had an eclair.

He ate cheese the day before he visited the Louvre and two days after seeing Sacre Coeur.

He visited the Louvre, Notre Dame, and Versailles on three days in a row.

The Louvre is closed on Tuesday. Les Invalides is open every day.

His weekend trips were to the Arc de Triomphe and Versailles.

He didn't eat gateau on Thursday or crepes on Tuesday.

He ate a croissant the day after he saw the Eiffel Tower.

HOLD ON TIGHT

Which of these seahorses is the odd one out?

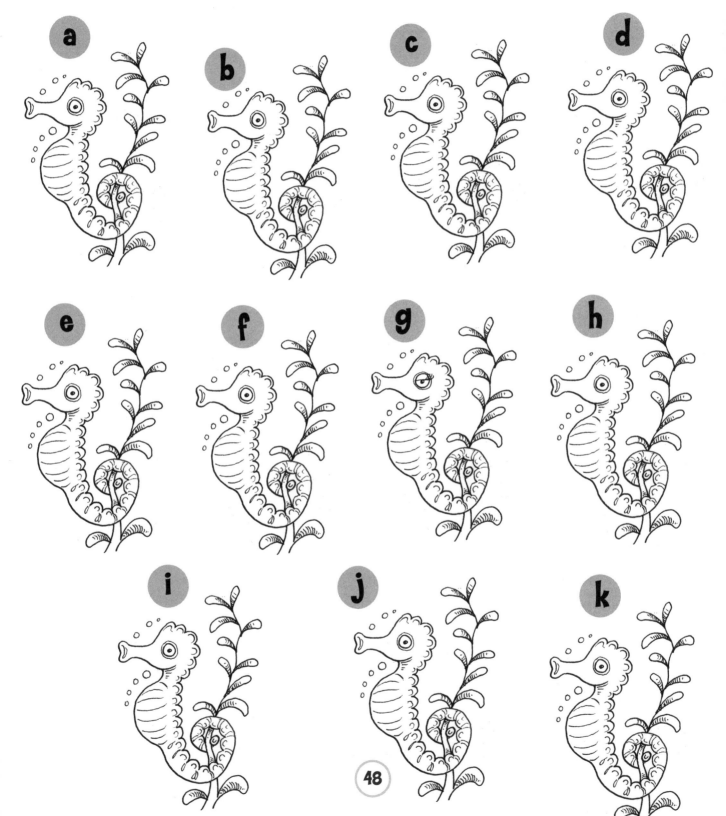

FROG PRINCE

Fill in the number pyramid to help the frog break the magic spell!
Simply add two numbers that are next to each other, and
write the answer above them.

HEAD IN THE CLOUDS

Can you design a brand new flying machine? Decide whether it has wings, or rotors, or maybe it's balloon powered? You're in charge!

DARTING AROUND

Each of these frogs has an identical match, apart from one.
Can you find the one on its own?

BOO!

Find a path to the pumpkin lantern, following the pictures in this order:

1  2 3

PET PICKUP

The owners have returned from their trip and want to collect their pets. Work out these calculations to enter the code number.

a $(14 \times 2) - 25$

b $16 \times \frac{1}{2}$

c $42 - (10 \times 4)$

d $100 \div 20$

SUPER SWIMMERS

Overwater and underwater, these penguins hurtle through the ocean!
Which of the small boxes is not part of the main picture?

CREATURES OF THE DEEP

Crack the code by moving one letter backward in the alphabet each time, to find the names of these unusual fish that live in the deepest parts of the ocean.

WJQFSGJTi

GBOHUPPUi

ESBHPOGJTi

iBUDiFUGGJTi

57

IN A MUDDLE

It's midnight, and Cinderella is in a fluster! Which group of letters is the only one that will spell her name properly?

REALNICENDL

RELCIDOLAN

RELCIDOLAN

DRICLEANLIE

CALLREDINE

DEARCLEANLI

AIR TRAFFIC CONTROL

Can you find ten differences between these two pictures?

BIRD'S EYE VIEW

What does this farm look like from above?

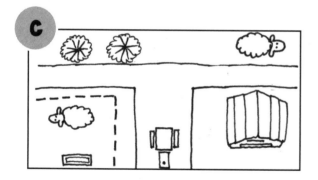

LIGHTS OUT

There are ten bedtime words hidden in
this grid: down, across, and diagonally.
Can you find them all?

YAWN   MOON
STORY   PILLOW
BLANKET   WHISPER
LULLABY   TORCH
TEDDY   DREAMS

S	M	A	E	R	D	B	M	O	T
L	P	W	H	I	L	O	Y	F	S
R	A	I	M	A	O	D	A	U	W
Y	T	S	L	N	E	D	W	L	H
R	E	O	O	L	K	Y	N	L	I
O	K	T	R	P	O	O	M	I	S
T	N	E	T	C	N	W	A	P	P
S	A	O	O	M	H	T	S	K	E
D	L	U	L	L	A	B	Y	E	R
D	B	S	T	E	D	D	Y	T	B

HIDING AWAY

How many dragonflies can you count in this beautiful Japanese garden?

WHAT AM I?

Work out which letters of the alphabet are missing to discover the name of the mystery sea creature. The clues might help you, too!

Q A N H I C J

G D Y P K

U V F

W X

Z

I have ten legs.

I am nocturnal.

I can live to be 100 years old!

My front claws are huge.

My blood is blue!

I walk around the sea floor but when I swim, I go backward!

GENIE-OUS

Are you clever enough to fill in the genie's grid? Each row, column, and mini-grid should have one of each picture in it.

AIR SHOW

These crazy pilots are entertaining the crowds below!
Which of the small boxes is not part of the main picture?

a b c d e

EAGLE ADDITION

Which is the only eagle whose numbers don't add up to 99?

SHINE A LIGHT

Write the correct number next to each picture, using the clues to help you. If you get them all right, each row, column, and diagonal will add up to 15.

1 They help you cross the road.

2 It has a face on it.

3 Used for celebrations.

4 Turn it out to sleep.

5 It uses light as a trap.

6 It's out of this world!

7 Don't touch this one.

8 A handy tool to have.

9 It's easily blown out.

SHADY SKYLINE

Which of the silhouettes is an exact match for
the amazing Guggenheim Museum in Bilbao, Spain?

I SEE SEA SHELLS

Can you spot one shell here that doesn't match any of the others?

✦ FAIRYTALE ENDING

How many words with three letters or more can you make from this phrase? There's one listed to get you started.

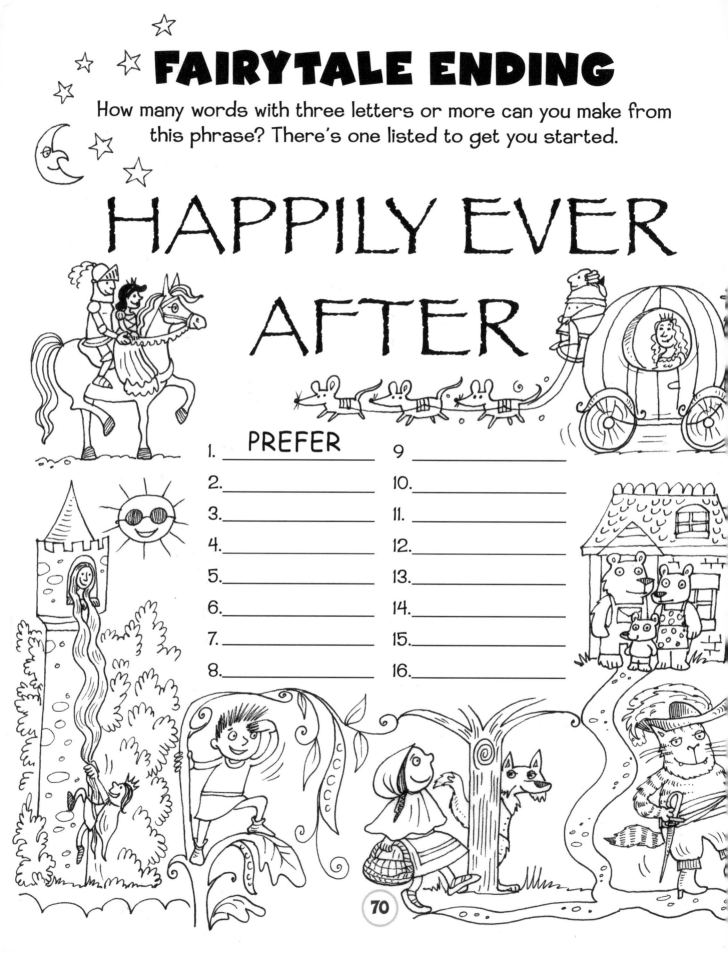

HAPPILY EVER AFTER

1. PREFER
2. _____
3. _____
4. _____
5. _____
6. _____
7. _____
8. _____
9. _____
10. _____
11. _____
12. _____
13. _____
14. _____
15. _____
16. _____

SCHOOL TRIP

Class 6B are having a day out. Can you tell which three pesky pupils have not made it back to the coach on time in the second picture?

EAT UP!

Cross out every other letter, starting with S, to reveal
a creature that eats with its head upside down!

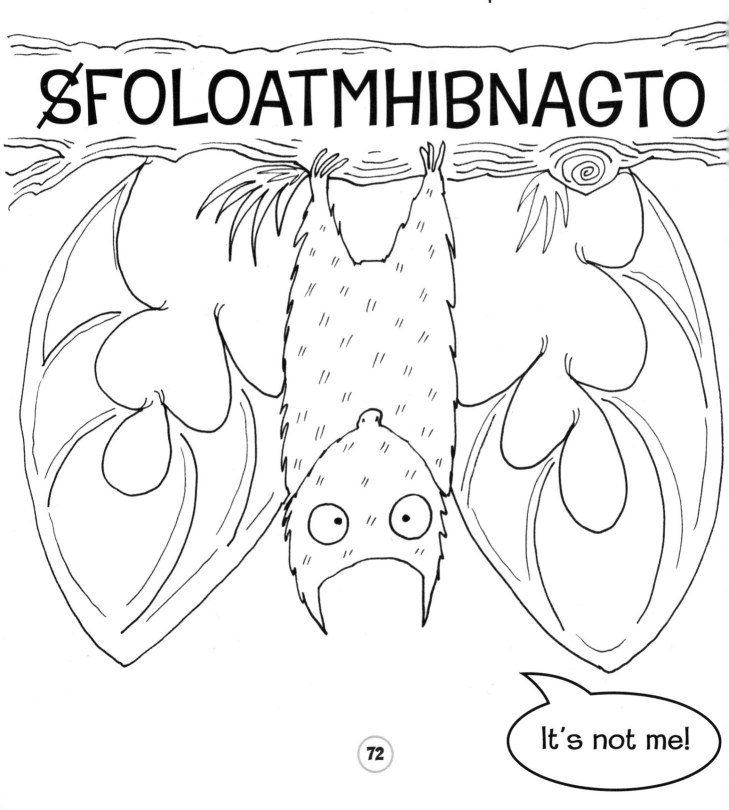

S̶FOLOATMHIBNAGTO

It's not me!

RICH WITCH

Use the logic clues to work out which witch is really rich.

The really rich witch is wearing a crooked hat.

She has curly hair.

The rich witch has a pointed nose.

She is holding a broom.

73

LOCH NESS

Which of these souvenirs from Scotland is the odd one out?

WHICH WHALE?

Work out which of these whales will grow the biggest
by doing the calculation on each one.

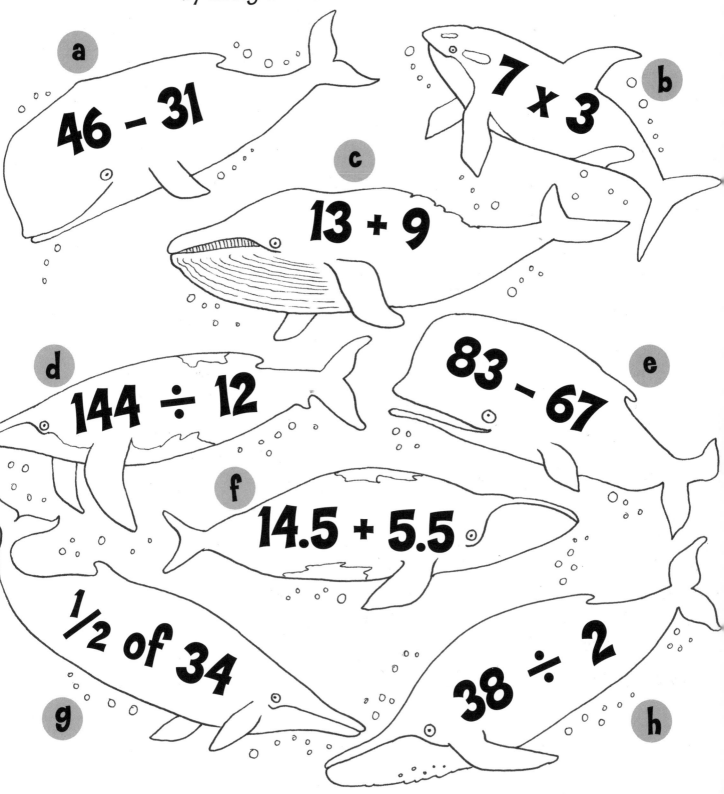

a   46 – 31

b   7 x 3

c   13 + 9

d   144 ÷ 12

e   83 – 67

f   14.5 + 5.5

g   1/2 of 34

h   38 ÷ 2

SWEET DREAMS

What is Sleeping Beauty dreaming about?
You decide! But please don't give her nightmares!

BUBBLE TROUBLE

Which two of these bubble cars are exactly the same?

a

b

c

d

e

f

g

h

i

j

k

l

HISS! WOOF! BAA!

Find a path from left to right, following the pictures in this order:

1   2   3

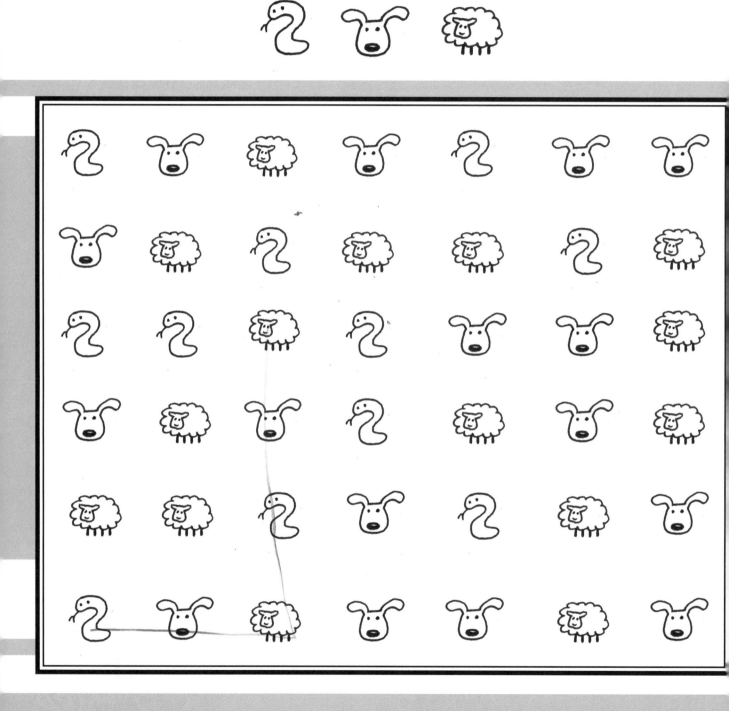

78

SLEEPOVER

Can you spot each of these items in the main picture?

WRITE ON

Use the letters in the grid to find out who wrote and published many of our best-loved fairy tales.

	1	2	3	4
a	G	R	O	U
b	L	i	C	M
c	A	B	T	E
d	N	S	P	H

c3 d4 c4   c2 a2 a3 c3 d4 c4 a2 d2

_ _ _   _ _ _ _ _ _ _ _

a1 a2 b2 b4 b4

_ _ _ _ _

PETS WIN PRIZES

Which pets have won the prizes in this show?
Let your imagination run wild!

AFRICAN ANTICS

Work out the answer to the joke using the special hieroglyphic code!

What would you get if you crossed the Nile and the Sahara?

LORD OF THE SEA

Which group of letters will not spell POSEIDON correctly?

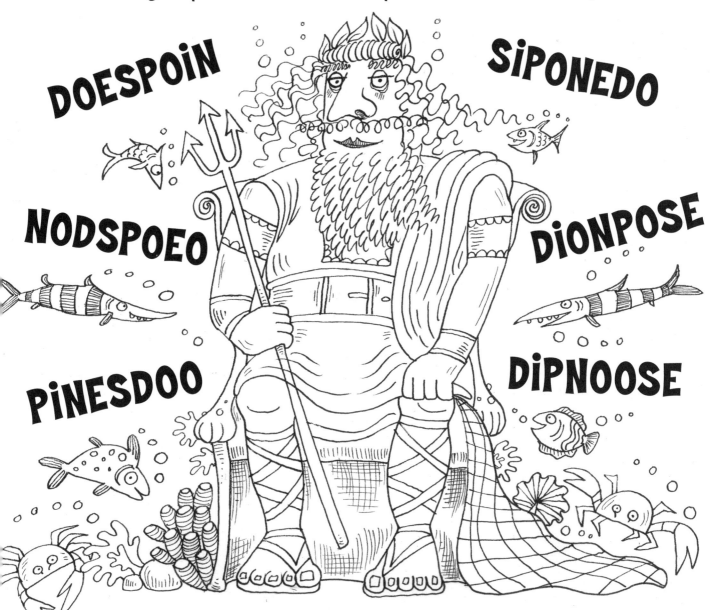

DOESPOIN

SIPONEDO

NODSPOEO

DIONPOSE

PINESDOO

DIPNOOSE

Did you know?

Poseidon was the Greek god of the sea. His golden palace was at the bottom of the ocean, with seaweed gardens and beautiful pearl decorations.

SLEEPY HEAD

Can you find ten differences between these two pictures?

ENGINE PROBLEM

Follow the cogs and pulleys to work out whether this machine will be switched on or off by pushing the handle to the left.

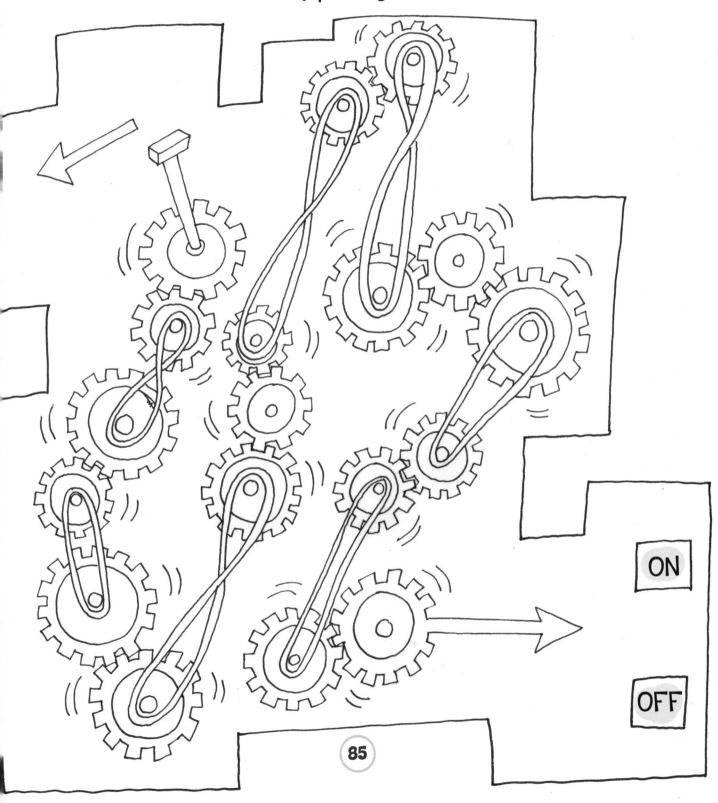

IN THE TREES

All ten animals that are hiding in this grid can usually be found in the trees. Look for their names across, down, and diagonally.

KOALA   PARROT   SLOTH

LEMUR   FROG   SQUIRREL

SNAKE   AYEAYE   MARMOSET

             GIBBON

S	Q	A	R	R	O	R	F	K	P
N	K	O	A	L	A	M	O	M	A
A	L	A	Y	E	S	Q	U	A	R
S	Q	U	I	R	R	E	L	R	I
F	K	O	A	E	E	R	T	M	Q
R	T	O	R	R	A	P	R	O	S
O	G	M	A	E	M	A	R	S	L
G	I	I	K	Y	L	Y	O	E	O
U	B	A	B	A	S	E	M	T	T
Q	N	G	I	B	B	Q	M	A	H
S	T	R	E	E	O	M	U	U	R
A	Y	E	A	Y	E	N	O	I	R

UNDER CANVAS

It's lights out on the campsite!
How many lanterns and torches can you count?

STARS AND STRIPES

Which letters of the alphabet are missing here?
Use them to spell the name of a state and popular vacation
destination in the southeastern United States.

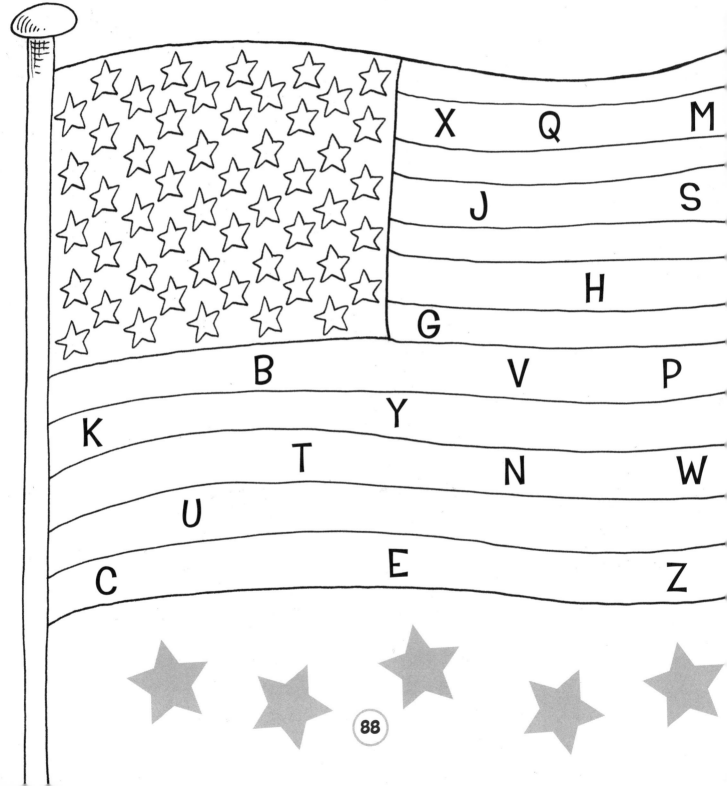

X   Q   M

J   S

H

G   V   P

B   Y

K   T   N   W

U

C   E   Z

SEA-DOKU

Fill in the grid so that each row, column, and mini-grid has one of each of the sea creatures in it.

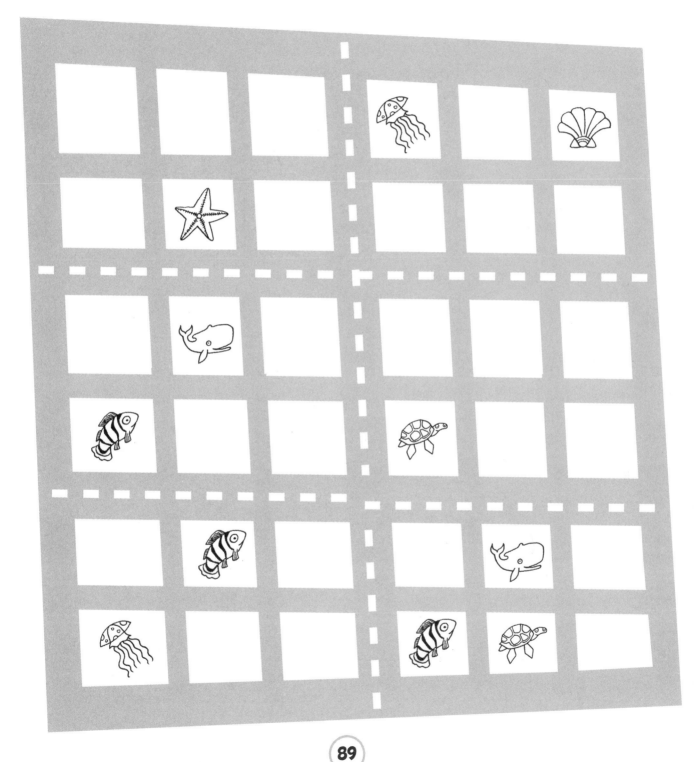

89

SWEET TREAT

Look what Hansel and Gretel have found in the forest!
Which three small boxes make up part of the main picture?

SKATER SUMS

Match each skater to his or her board by doing the arithmetic.

49

38

76 ÷ 2

14 x 3

42

36

23 + 26

35

52 – 17

9 x 4

CREATURE FEATURES

Write the correct number next to each picture, using the clues to help you. If you get them all right, each row, column, and diagonal will add up to 15.

1 It has no legs.

2 A common pet.

3 He's full of bounce!

4 This one isn't real.

5 It weighs a ton!

6 Swings through the trees.

7 Watch out for its tail.

8 Most at home in the water.

9 A hooded reptile.

SHADY LADY

Which one of the silhouettes is an exact match for Izzy the witch?

SQUARE EYES

Can you find this mini-grid, made up of number symbols used in some parts of India, hidden in the large grid?

DEEP THOUGHTS

How many words with three letters or more can you make from this phrase? There's one listed to get you started.

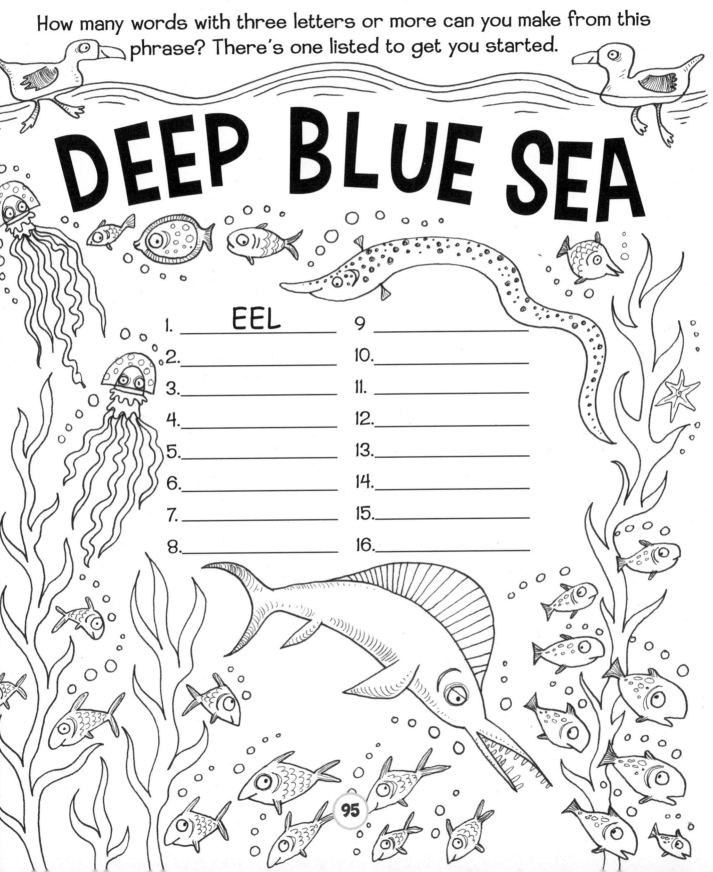

DEEP BLUE SEA

1. EEL
2. _____
3. _____
4. _____
5. _____
6. _____
7. _____
8. _____

9. _____
10. _____
11. _____
12. _____
13. _____
14. _____
15. _____
16. _____

FOREST FUN

The woodland creatures are playing hide and seek. Can you see three of them in the top picture who have hidden away in the bottom picture?

RACEY TRACEY

Cross out the letters that appear more than once to find out which of these vehicles Tracey wants to race.

97

SNAIL'S PACE

Use the logic clues to work out which child owns each snail,
and in what order they finish in the race.

a

c

Katie's snail has stripes.

The biggest snail doesn't win.

Maggie's snail beats Leo's.

The snail with the pointed shell
comes last.

b

	1st	2nd	3rd
KATIE			
LEO			
MAGGIE			

	A	B	C
KATIE			
LEO			
MAGGIE			

SHINING BRIGHT

One of these stars is different from all the others. Can you find it?

ALL MIXED UP

Mr South has messed up his geography lesson and needs to piece together these country names. Can you help him?

BOTS

PARA

ARIA

BULG

LAND

OPIA

MONG

UGAL

SCOT

AKIA

ETHI

GUAY

PORT

OLIA

SLOV

WANA

DIVE DRIVE

Design a vehicle that can go underwater. Will it be a submarine, or a land vehicle that can adapt to the ocean?

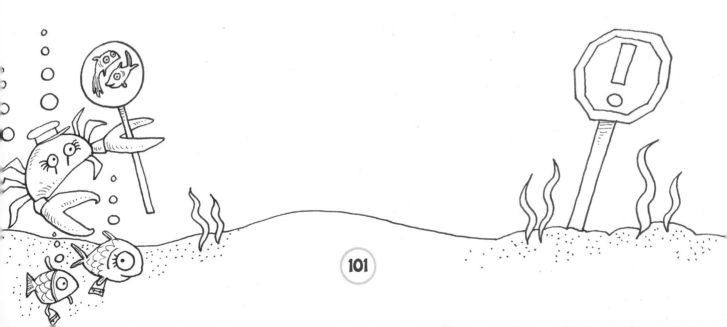

NIGHT SHIFT

The elves are busy in the workshop, helping the shoemaker overnight.
They have made lots of pairs of shoes, but three of them have no match.
Which three are they?

102

RACING HOME

Follow the arrows to find a way to the finish line, moving the number of spaces written in the arrow each time.

START

FINISH

STANDING STONES

Which of the stones at Stonehenge weighs the most?
Work out the calculations on each to find out.

$7 \times 8 \div 2$

Half of 58

1/3 of 99

48×0.5

15×3

$27 + 29$

6×7

JUNGLE JAPES

Can you spot each of the circled items in the main picture?

SCARY STORY

Use the letters in the grid to solve the clues.

	1	2	3	4
a	M	N	A	V
b	W	B	L	E
c	Y	O	T	P
d	S	R	i	K

The author of the book "Dracula"

b2 d2 a3 a1   d1 c3 c2 d4 b4 d2

B R A M   S T O K E R

The part of Romania where Count Dracula lives

c3 d2 a3 a2 d1 c1 b3 a4 a3 a2 d3 a3

T _ _ _ _ _ _ _ _ _ _ _

DESIGNER WHEELS

How would you customize this car to make it stand out from the crowd?

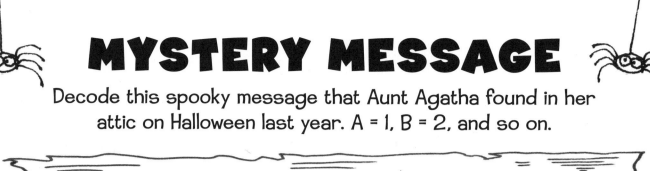

MYSTERY MESSAGE

Decode this spooky message that Aunt Agatha found in her attic on Halloween last year. A = 1, B = 2, and so on.

4 15 14 ' 20

DON T

8 1 22 5

HAVE

14 9 7 8 20 13 1 18 5 19 !

NIGHTMARES

CAPITAL LETTERS

Unscramble each of the sets of letters to find a country, and then match it to the correct capital city.

SIRUSA

KIPANAST

BGIUELM

GECREE

DANCAA

DOLPAN

LASTURAIA

RYWANO

Canberra

Brussels

Ottawa

Athens

Oslo

Islamabad

Moscow

Warsaw

LOST CITY

Study these two pictures of the lost city of Atlantis carefully.
Can you spot ten differences?

A PRINCELY PALACE

Look at the picture of the Frog Prince's palace gardens. Can you see which of the smaller pictures is how it would look from above?

a
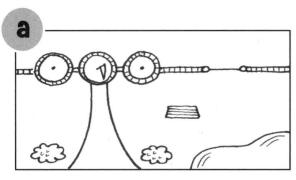

b
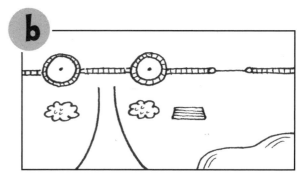

c
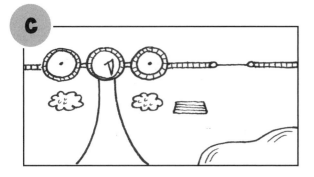

d
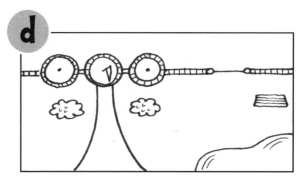

e
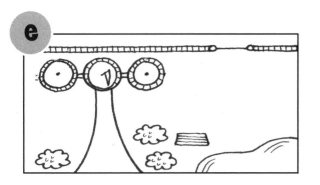

f
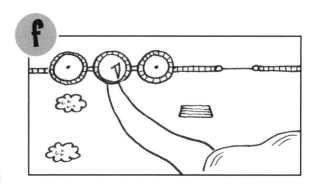

111

FAST OR SLOW?

Most, but not all, of these words are hidden in the grid.
Which are there more of: speedy words or slow ones?

RUN　　　ZOOM　　　WALK　　　RAMBLE
DASH　　SPRINT　　CRAWL　　SAUNTER
GALLOP　RUSH　　　MARCH　　CREEP
JOG　　　SCUTTLE　STEP　　　LOITER

R P S C U T T L E S S
Z U G A L L O P S A
L I S J D M A R P U
O R N H A W A L R N
i O U T S W Z O i T
T C M N H G A L N E
E R A M B L E L T R
R A G S A U N J K J
E W S T E P Z O O M
T L M A R C H G P S

BIRD WORLD

It's busy on the boating lake! How many ducklings can you count?

SHY GUY

Use the missing letters of the alphabet to spell a creature that lives on every continent, and usually comes out at night.

FNPQSARBGDXYHETCUVIJKMZ

FLYING THE FLAG

Fill in the grid so that each row, column, and
mini-grid has one of each flag in it.

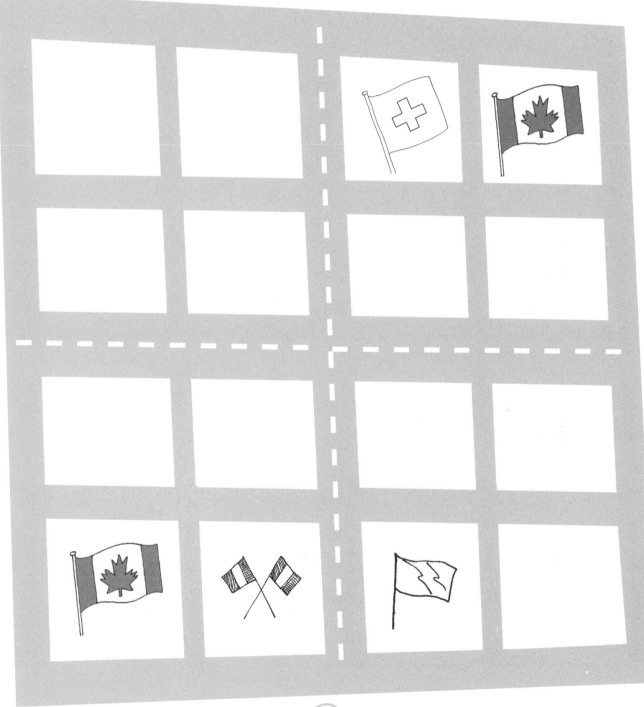

FIT FOR A KING

Can you spot each of these items in the main picture?

THE GOLDEN GOOSE

Fill in the numbers on the goose's golden eggs by adding two numbers that are next to each other, and writing the answer above, or by taking a number away from the one above it.

10

20 27

9

16

117

ON THE MOVE

Write the correct number next to each picture, using the clues to help you. If you get them all right, each row, column, and diagonal will add up to 15.

1 It has handlebars but no engine
2 A two-wheeled vehicle
3 Take it out on the ocean
4 It is powered by the wind
5 A flying machine
6 It can go on the water or in the air
7 A vehicle for lots of passengers
8 Pedal powered!
9 Keep on truckin'!

STAY AWAY

Which one of these silhouettes is an exact match for the main picture?

SEEING STARS

Can you find this mini-grid hidden in the large grid?

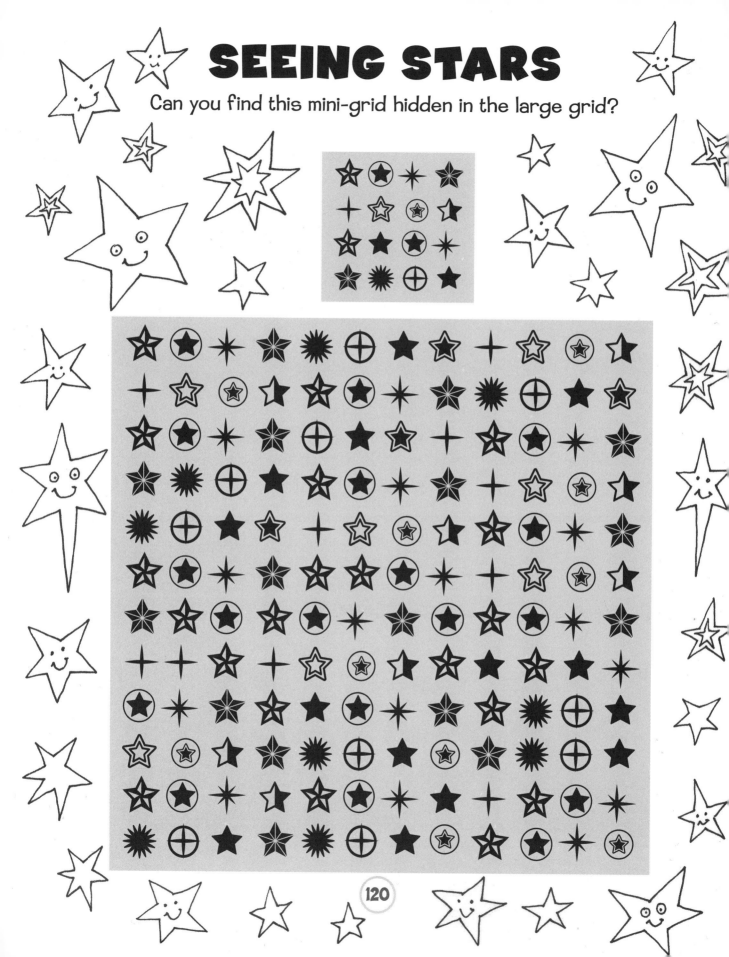

AROUND THE WORLD

How many words with three letters or more can you make from this phrase? There's one listed to get you started.

SEEING THE SIGHTS

1. SHINE
2. _____
3. _____
4. _____
5. _____
6. _____
7. _____
8. _____
9. _____
10. _____

11. _____
12. _____
13. _____
14. _____
15. _____
16. _____
17. _____
18. _____
19. _____
20. _____

SOMETHING FISHY

Five creatures have disappeared in the second picture.
Can you spot which ones?

LOCKED AWAY

Which lock of Rapunzel's magic hair should the Prince climb to rescue her from the tower?

123

CRAZY RACERS

Toilet races are a popular pastime in the USA and Australia!
Use the clues to work out who is the winner in this loo-natic race.

The winner is not wearing a tie.

First place goes to a driver with a black helmet.

The winner is wearing trainers.

A person in a T-shirt is first over the finish line.

FOOT FRENZY

One of these footprints is different from all the others. Can you find it?

THE SKY AT NIGHT

Which of the alien ships has come from the galaxy farthest away?
Add up the numbers to find out which equals the most.

16
5
43
9
26
4

12
4
27
16
31
8

18
7
31
13
28
3

YOU RULE!

Imagine you are the leader of your own country. Design a flag and a matching sports kit with any patterns or symbols you like.

127

SEA SLUGS

Look at these crazy creatures! Many of them have an identical twin, but three of them do not. Can you spot the soloists?

YOU CAN'T CATCH ME!

Help the Gingerbread Man run from the top row to the bottom row, by jumping on the cookies in the correct order:

MOVING HOUSE

Can you find each of the listed items in the main picture?

CRITICAL LIST

Use the letters in the grid to solve the clues and find two animal species that are in serious danger of becoming extinct.

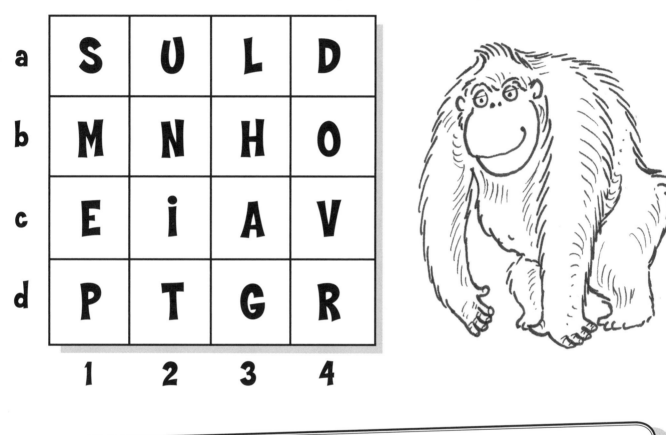

	1	2	3	4
a	S	U	L	D
b	M	N	H	O
c	E	i	A	V
d	P	T	G	R

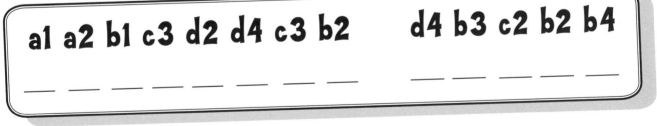

a1 a2 b1 c3 d2 d4 c3 b2   d4 b3 c2 b2 b4

___ ___ ___ ___ ___ ___ ___ ___   ___ ___ ___ ___ ___

b1 b4 a2 b2 d2 c3 c2 b2   d3 b4 d4 c2 a3 a3 c3

___ ___ ___ ___ ___ ___ ___ ___   ___ ___ ___ ___ ___ ___ ___

MOON PORTRAIT

What do you think the man in the moon looks like?
Draw him here, or make a woman in the moon, if you prefer!

LOOK AT ME!

Move one letter back in the alphabet each time to decode the message, so C = B, B = A, and so on. It will tell you what this bird is called and how it attracts a mate!

UiF CMVF GPPUFE CPPCZ EBODFT

___ ____ _____ _____ _____

UP TiPX JUT GBCVMPVT GFFU!

__ ____ ___ _____ ____!

133

ALL FALL DOWN

Can you spot ten differences between these
two pictures of Niagara Falls in North America?

BIG LAUGHS

Follow the instructions to find the answer to the joke.

Cross out any words containing S.

Lose the words that end with CH.

Get rid of any words beginning with F.

Why did the whale swim across the ocean?

TO TEACH SWIM

FISH FETCH GET

FIND FAR

SAND REACH SOME FAT

TO FROM

THE OTHER

BEACH FOLLOW

FRIGHTENED SEA

SHARK TIDE SHORE

136

HAVING A BALL

Find all of the words from the story of Cinderella, hidden in the grid.
They can appear across, down or diagonally.

SLIPPER **MIDNIGHT**

CINDERS **BALLGOWN**

SISTER **PUMPKIN**

UGLY **CARRIAGE**

FAIRY **PRINCE**

P	C	U	G	C	N	E	S	L	i	P	P
i	i	S	B	A	L	L	G	O	W	N	G
L	E	i	D	R	M	i	E	M	i	D	B
S	L	S	R	R	U	L	N	A	S	P	A
U	i	S	L	i	P	P	E	R	Y	U	L
G	F	S	E	A	L	U	D	L	L	M	L
L	A	M	T	G	U	M	G	E	A	P	A
G	i	i	R	E	G	U	P	U	M	K	i
O	R	D	C	A	R	B	A	L	L	i	R
W	Y	M	i	D	N	i	G	H	T	N	A
N	C	A	R	R	P	R	i	N	C	E	C
L	C	i	N	D	E	R	S	S	i	S	T

WE ARE SAILING

It's regatta week and the seas are teeming with sailors!
How many fish can you spot in this scene?

REPTILE RIDDLER

Use the missing letters of the alphabet in each section to spell the names of some of the world's most fascinating snakes.

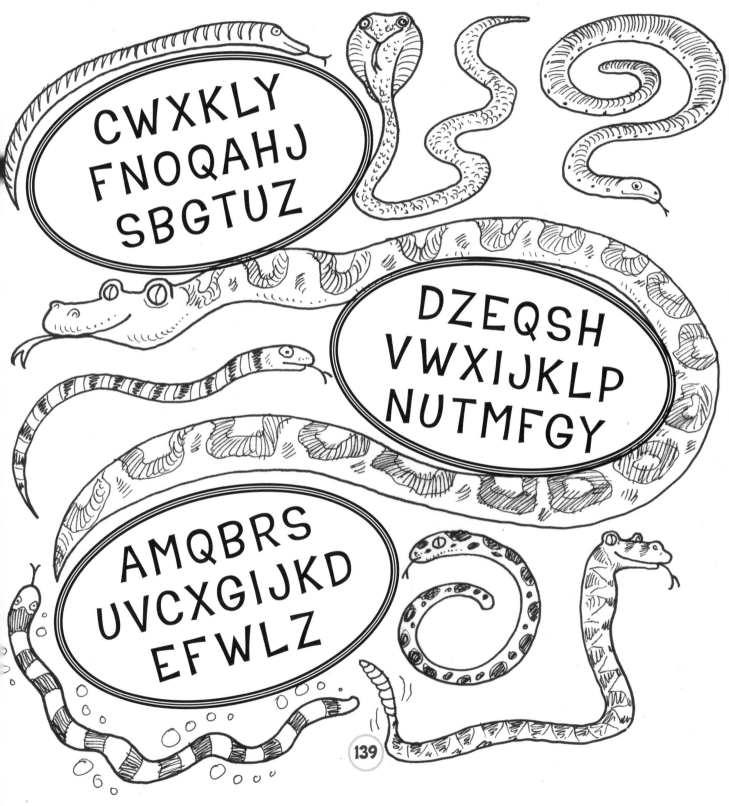

CWXKLY
FNOQAHJ
SBGTUZ

DZEQSH
VWXIJKLP
NUTMFGY

AMQBRS
UVCXGIJKD
EFWLZ

WHO-DOKU

Who's hiding in the dark?! Fill in the grid so that each row, column, and mini-grid has one of each pair of eyes.

140

CARNIVAL!

Rio de Janeiro in Brazil is famous for its carnival.
Which three small boxes make up part of the main picture?

a   b   c   d   e

MER-PETS

Find out which pet belongs to each mermaid by doing the calculations and matching them to the correct answer.

a
48

9 x 5

b
42

6 x 7

11 x 4

8 x 6

44

45

c

d

STORY TIME

Write the correct number next to each picture, using the clues to help you. If you get them all right, each row, column, and diagonal will add up to 15.

1 She pricked her finger and fell asleep.

2 He will grant you three wishes.

3 He turns straw into gold!

4 He needs a kiss to break the spell.

5 Run, run, as fast as you can!

6 Their fur is pure white.

7 They like porridge for breakfast.

8 A fire-breathing beast.

9 He'll huff and puff and blow your house down.

VINTAGE WHEELS

Which of these silhouettes is an exact match for the main picture?

SPOTTED

Look carefully and you will "spot" one creeping cat
that is slightly different from the rest.

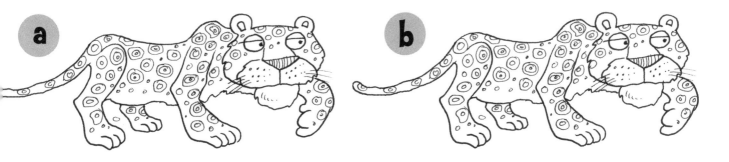

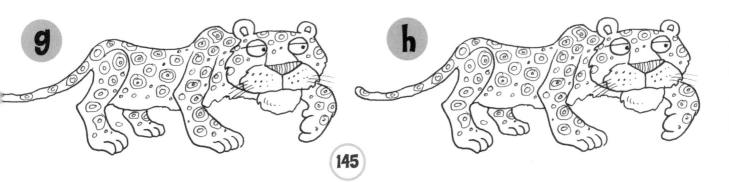

SNEAKY SNACKS

How many words can you make from the letters in the phrase below?

MIDNIGHT FEAST

1. SING
2. _____
3. _____
4. _____
5. _____
6. _____
7. _____
8. _____
9. _____
10. _____
11. _____
12. _____
13. _____
14. _____
15. _____
16. _____

IN RUINS

Which of the tourists are missing in the second picture?

GOING DOWN

Cross out every other letter, starting with W,
to find the sport being done here.

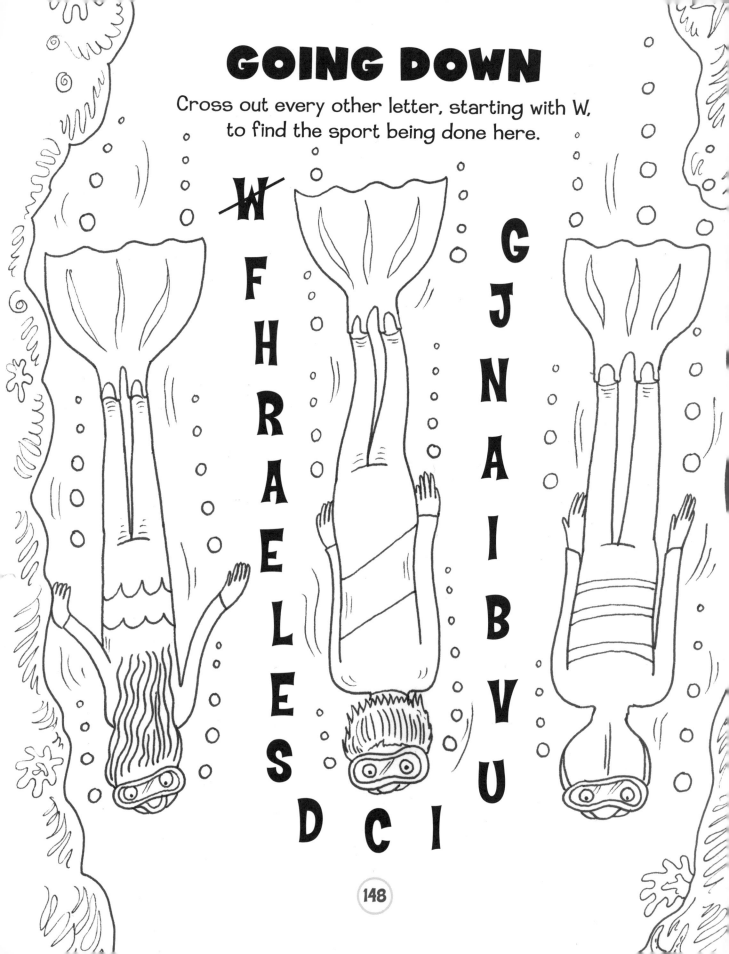

~~W~~ F H R A E L E S D C I J N A I B V U G

THREE LITTLE PIGS

Use the clues to work out which pig lives in each house.

A male pig lives in the house made of straw.

The female pig does not own the house made of sticks.

The pig wearing a tie does not own the house made of straw.

DIGGING IT

One of these machines is a tiny bit different
from the rest. Can you spot it?

a

b

c

d

e

f

g

h

i

PAIR UP A PENGUIN

Give each penguin a partner by finding the pairs
that have the same answers.

5 x 3

10.5 + 7.5

35 - 14

9 x 2

1/5 x 100

3 x 7

40 x 0.5

30 ÷ 2

SCAREDY CAT

Something has spooked poor Pusskin.
Draw the scariest monster you can imagine.

HEADS YOU WIN

Which one of these Easter Island statues does not have a twin?

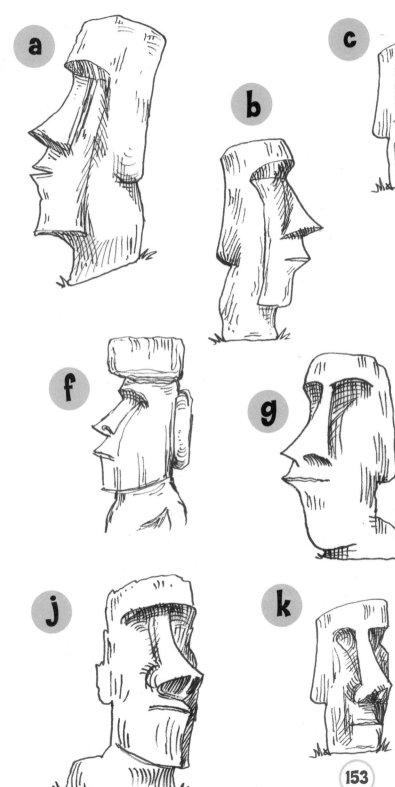

FOLLOW THAT FISH!

Find a way from the top of the grid to the bottom,
following the fish in this order:

1   2   3

THE TOTALLY BRILLIANT
WORLD
OF
PUZZLES

ANSWERS

3 ON SURFARI

8 TRICK OR TREAT

9 JUST FOR LAUGHS
Because it can't sit down!

10 NO FISH

4 SHARK ATTACK
Bull shark, great white, tiger shark

6 SUPER SPEED
Bugatti Veyron

7 ON THE LOOKOUT
EATMARK, TREMERKA

P	E	S	U	R	L	A	W	C	F	N	W
D	A	N	E	M	O	N	E	R	O	A	A
U	P	E	D	T	T	W	A	R	H	N
G	E	P	O	S	E	H	A	A	T	E
i	H	C	T	P	T	T	O	O	N
M	G	R	O	E	T	O	S	O
P	O	T	H	E	N	L	D	T	S	S	C
E	i	T	G	L	N	A	C	U	T	H	U
S	N	O	B	T	T	E	N	R	G	R	T
Q	M	A	N	T	i	S	S	E	A	P
U	R	S	Q	U	i	D	E	Q	M	H	E
C	S	A	E	C	O	R	A	L	U	P	N

11   MISCHIEF MAKING
There are 15 ice creams.

12   MISSING PARTS
MOPED

13   ZOO-DOKU

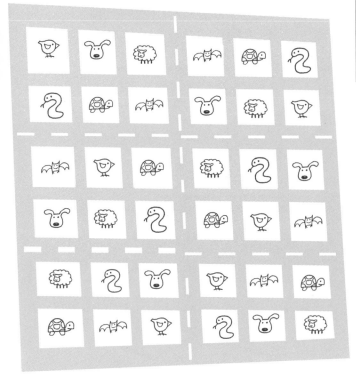

14   HAUNTED HOUSE
c

15   AUSSIE ARITHMETIC
d

16   OCEAN EXPLORER

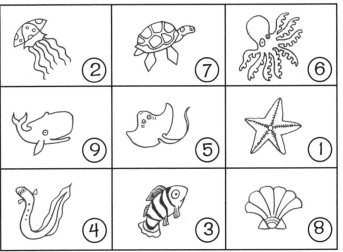

17   SPINNING GOLD
e

18   A SCREW LOOSE

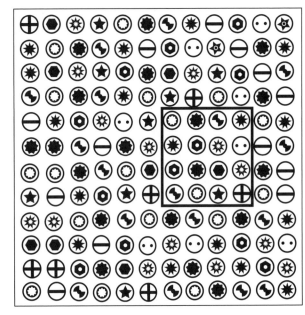

19 WALKiES!

Here are some you might have found: move, dome, olive, good, ivy, mood, mole, gloomy, evil, oil.

20 SPOOKY SCENE

21 BUILDING BRIDGES

a = New York
b = Sydney
c = London
d = China

22 LOViNG THE WAVES

Estelle goes jet skiing and is from Australia.
Floyd does wind surfing and is from the USA.
Cara is a scuba diver and is from Greece.

23 MYSTiCAL CREATURES

j

24 ZOOM!

69 + 31
35 + 65
74 + 26
58 + 42
86 + 14
78 + 22

26 BOOM!

f

27 SLOWLY DOES iT

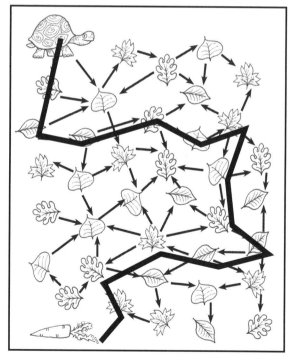

28 TREASURE TROVE

29 STEP UP
CHICHEN ITZA, MAYAS, YUCATAN

31 FIGHTING DRAGONS
ENGLAND, EGYPT, ISRAEL, ETHIOPIA, PORTUGAL, INDIA, UKRAINE

32 ON YOUR BIKE

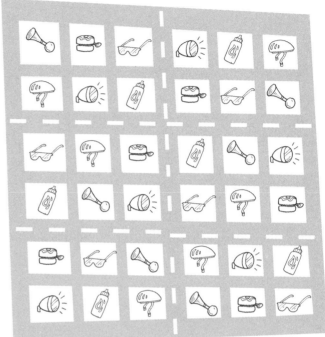

33 KING OF THE JUNGLE

34 LIGHTS OUT
Cut the striped wire

35 TOUR OF THE EAST

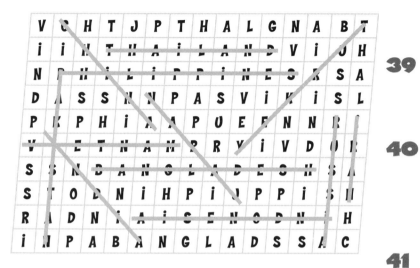

36 SHIPWRECKED

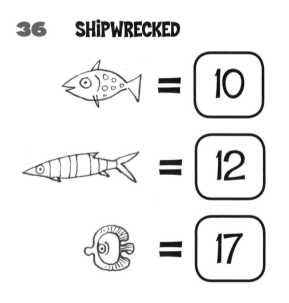

Fish = 10

Fish = 12

Fish = 17

37 DO YOU BELIEVE?

ELF, OGRE, IMP, GNOME

38 AIR RESCUE

ROPETHLICE = HELICOPTER

39 I HERD THAT!

a, c and e

40 GOING BATTY

2 bats: b and e

41 MAGIC SQUARE

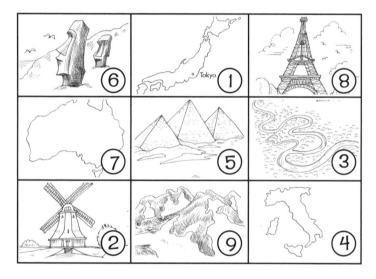

42 SUPER SUB

d

43   DRINK ME!

44   OFF ROADING

Here are some you might have found: few, hour, flour, whoever, feel, flew, where, whole, evil, fuel.

45   MORE AND MORE

46   IN THE DARK
WINTER SOLSTICE

47   FRENCH TRIP
MONDAY
Sacre Coeur, mousse
TUESDAY
Les Invalides, gateau
WEDNESDAY
Eiffel Tower, cheese
THURSDAY
The Louvre, croissant
FRIDAY
Notre Dame, crepes
SATURDAY
Versailles, tarte tatin
SUNDAY
Arc de Triomphe, eclair

48   HOLD ON TIGHT
g

49   FROG PRINCE

51 DARTING ABOUT

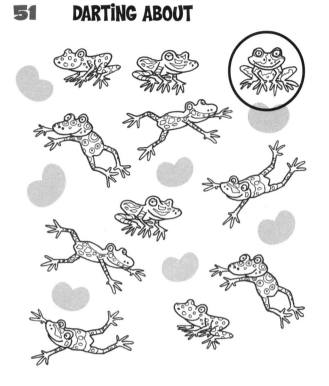

52 BOO!

53 PET PICKUP
3825

54 SUPER SWIMMERS
b

55 HERE WE GO
RICKSHAW

57 CREATURES OF THE DEEP
VIPERFISH, FANGTOOTH,
DRAGONFISH, HATCHETFISH

58 IN A MUDDLE
CALLREDINE = CINDERELLA

59 AIR TRAFFIC CONTROL

60   BIRD'S EYE VIEW
d

61   LIGHTS OUT

62   HIDING AWAY
15 dragonflies

63   WHAT AM I?
LOBSTER

64   GENIE-OUS

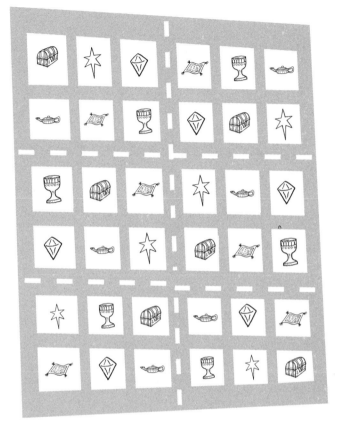

65   AIR SHOW
a

66   EAGLE ADDITION
c

67 SHINE A LIGHT

68 SHADY SKYLINE

c

69 I SEE SEA SHELLS

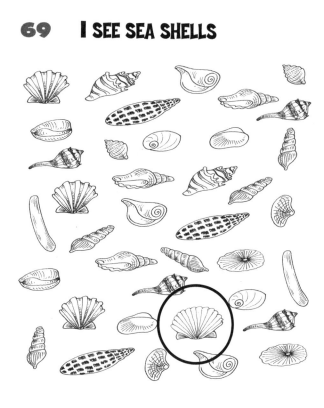

70 FAIRYTALE ENDING

Here are some you might have found: flip, alive, paper, rave, live, appear, faith, have, apple, river.

71 SCHOOL TRIP

72 EAT UP!

FLAMINGO

73 RICH WITCH

b

74 LOCH NESS

d

75 WHICH WHALE?

c

77 BUBBLE TROUBLE
c and i

78 HISS! WOOF! BAA!

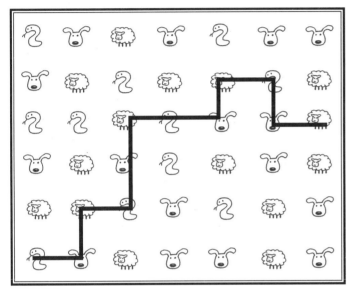

80 WRITE ON
THE BROTHERS GRIMM

82 AFRICAN ANTICS
Wet and thirsty!

83 LORD OF THE SEA
NODSPOEO

84 SLEEPY HEAD

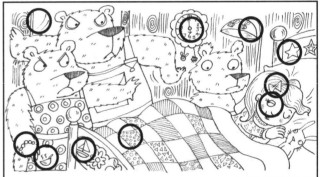

79 SLEEPOVER

85 ENGINE PROBLEM
Off

86 IN THE TREES

87 UNDER CANVAS
5 lanterns, 10 torches

88 STARS AND STRIPES
FLORIDA

89 SEA-DOKU

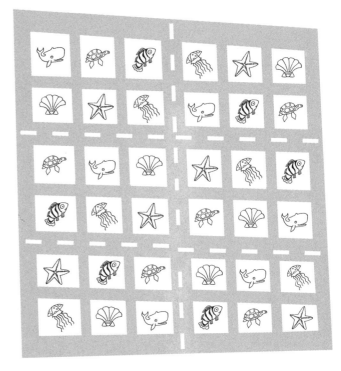

90 SWEET TREAT
a, d and e

91 SKATER SUMS
76 ÷ 2 = 38
14 x 3 = 42
23 + 26 = 49
52 - 17 = 35
9 x 4 = 36

92 CREATURE FEATURES

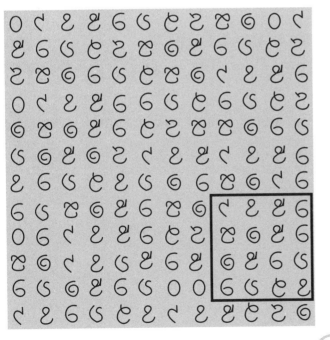

93 SHADY LADY

e

94 SQUARE EYES

95 DEEP THOUGHTS

Here are some you might have found: use, bleed, ape, pulse, asleep, base, easel, pause, sale, able.

96 FOREST FUN

97 RACEY TRACEY

SEGWAY

98 SNAIL'S PACE

Katie owns snail b which came first.
Leo owns snail a which came last.
Maggie owns snail c which came second.

99 SHINING BRIGHT

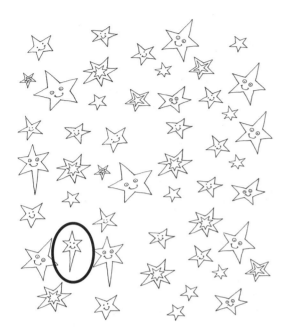

100 ALL MIXED UP

BOTSWANA, BULGARIA,
MONGOLIA, SCOTLAND, ETHIOPIA,
PORTUGAL, SLOVAKIA, PARAGUAY

102 NIGHT SHIFT

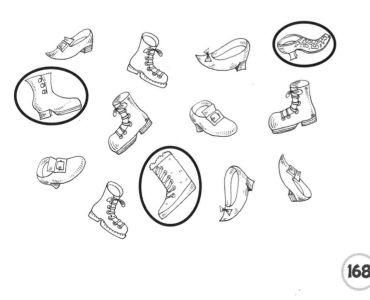

103 RACING HOME

104 STANDING STONES

27 + 29 [= 56]

105 JUNGLE JAPES

106 SCARY STORY

The author of the book 'Dracula' is Bram Stoker. The part of Romania where Count Dracula lives is Transylvania.

108 MYSTERY MESSAGE

DON'T HAVE NIGHTMARES!

109 CAPITAL LETTERS

Canberra AUSTRALIA
Brussels BELGIUM
Ottawa CANADA
Athens GREECE
Oslo NORWAY
Islamabad PAKISTAN
Moscow RUSSIA
Warsaw POLAND

110 LOST CITY

111 A PRINCELY PALACE

c

112 FAST OR SLOW?

There are more speedy words.

113 BIRD WORLD

25

114 SHY GUY

OWL

115   FLYING THE FLAG

117   THE GOLDEN GOOSE

116   FIT FOR A KING

118   ON THE MOVE

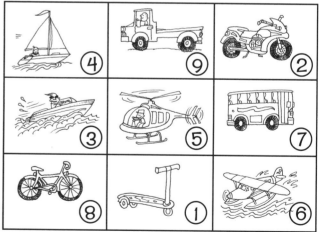

170

119 STAY AWAY

c

120 SEEING STARS

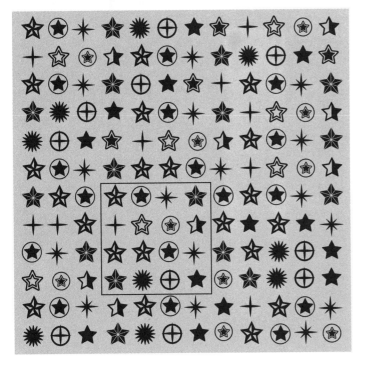

121 AROUND THE WORLD

Here are some you might have found: highest, hinge, these, eighth, test, hen, sigh, sing, sheet, sting.

122 SOMETHING FISHY

123 LOCKED AWAY

g

124 CRAZY RACERS

d

125 FOOT FRENZY

129 YOU CAN'T CATCH ME

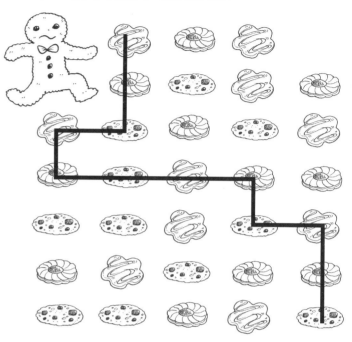

126 THE SKY AT NiGHT
The one on the left:
$$16 + 5 + 43 + 9 + 26 + 4 = 103$$

128 SEA SLUGS

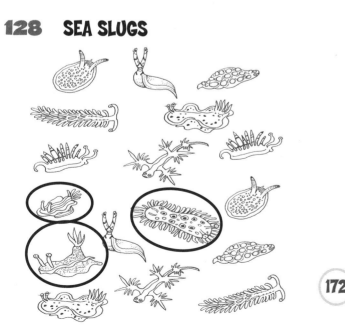

130 MOViNG HOUSE

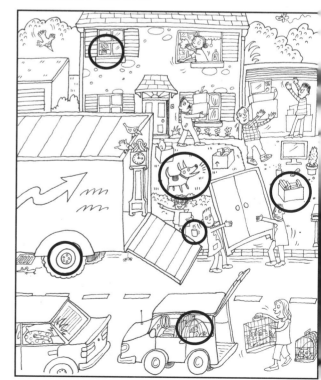

131 CRITICAL LIST
SUMATRAN RHINO, MOUNTAIN
GORILLA

133 LOOK AT ME!
THE BLUE FOOTED BOOBY
DANCES TO SHOW ITS
FABULOUS FEET!

134 ZAPPED
NHTLINING

135 ALL FALL DOWN

136 BIG LAUGHS
TO GET TO THE OTHER TIDE!

137 HAVING A BALL

P	C	U	G	C	N	E	S	L	i	P	P
i	i	S	B	A	L	L	C	C	W	H	G
L	E	i	D	R	M	i	E	M	i	D	B
S	L	S	R	U	L	N	A	S	P	A	
U	i	S	L	i	P	P	E	R	Y	U	L
G	i	S	E	A	L	U	D	i	L	M	L
L	A	M	T	G	U	M	C	E	A	P	A
G	i	R	F	G	U	P	U	M	K	i	
O	R	D	C	A	R	B	A	L	L	i	R
W	Y	M	i	D	N	i	G	H	T	N	A
N	C	A	R	R	P	R	i	N	C	E	C
L	G	i	N	D	E	R	S	S	i	S	T

138 WE ARE SAILING
There are 15 fish (not including
the shark fin in the water!).

173

139 REPTILE RIDDLER
VIPER, COBRA, PYTHON

140 WHO-DOKU

141 CARNIVAL!
a, c and d

142 MER-PETS
a = 8 x 6
b = 6 x 7
c = 11 x 4
d = 9 x 5

143 STORY TIME

144 VINTAGE WHEELS
d

145 SPOTTED
e

146 SNEAKY SNACKS

Here are some you might have found: fish, midget, hinge, fish, gift, fight, then, anthem, dig, thief.

147 IN RUiNS

148 GOiNG DOWN

FREE DIVING

149 THREE LiTTLE PiGS

Pig 2 lives in the house made of straw.

Pig 1 owns the house made of sticks.

Pig 3 has the house made of bricks.

150 DiGGiNG iT

g

151 PAiR UP A PENGUiN

5 x 3 = 30 ÷ 2
35 - 14 = 3 x 7
9 x 2 = 10.5 + 7.5
1/5 x 100 = 40 x 0.5

153 HEADS YOU WiN

g

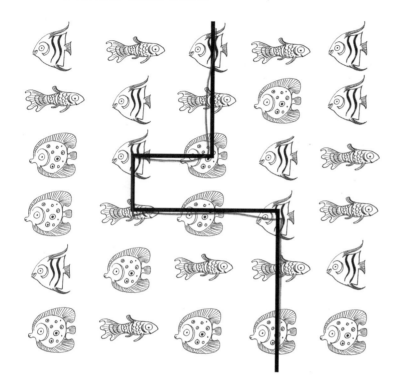